Stop to Smell the Roses

A Collection of Poems about Life

by

Claire Baker

(married, thirty-something, with children & working)

PepperPot Press
Market Drayton, UK

First published July 2007 by PepperPot Press, Market Drayton, UK.

This (colour) edition, incorporating additional and revised illustrations including full colour photographs, published November 2007 by PepperPot Press, Market Drayton UK.

ISBN: 978-0-9556408-1-0

Illustrations acknowledged under 'Table of Photographs and Illustrations'.

A CIP catalogue record for this book is available from the British Library.

Printed and bound by Think Ink, Ipswich, Suffolk, UK.

Foreword

I hope that you will find inside
A poem that you'll treasure,
Something that you'll want to read
That gives you lots of pleasure.

There's a poem to read on Father's Day,
And one to read on Mother's,
Something for a Funeral,
And a few significant others...

There's a poem to make you laugh,
And a poem to make you cry,
A poem to raise your spirits,
Another to wonder why.

Mostly, one to make you appreciate
The precious Gift of Life,
And to keep in mind its beauty
Throughout hardship or strife.

*

Acknowledgements

Thanks to...

My husband and the father of my children

for being the inspiration behind the poems highlighting some of the differences between men and women, and for his huge contribution to parenthood – *'For Everything You Do, Dad'* was written for him.

My children

for being the inspiration behind all the poems about parenthood, and for making me appreciate so many things about life that I forgot as I grew up.

My mother, my grandmother, and my children's grandparents

for being the inspiration behind the poem *'Where are You, Nanny?'* which is probably my favourite poem of this collection.

My parents

for always supporting me in everything I do. You have given me so much.

My sister

for always believing in me and for encouraging me to publish this book.

My friend Kate

for taking time to read through the collection and give me feedback.

Auntie Angela

for unwittingly giving advice that provided the title of this book.

Leanne

for her encouragement during the compilation of the original book.

Judith, and other friends and family who encouraged me along the way.

God

for many things, including a loving and supportive family, and especially the Gift of children.

I count myself very lucky.

Table of Photographs & Illustrations

21. Photograph of Abalone Cove sunset – Dan Parsons / www.studiodrp.com.

22. Drawing of child in meadow with butterfly in the sky – Phil Burton.

23. Photograph of Scot's pine with mist and sunbeams – Mark Taylor / Warren Photographic.

24. Photograph of sunset – Galyna Andrushko / Dreamstime.com.

25. Photograph of rose used on 'Epilogue' page – Robson Bolam.

26. Photograph of a section of the Dingle, Shrewsbury, England – Robson Bolam.

27. Back cover photograph of mist and sunbeams in the New Forest, Hampshire, England – Mark Taylor / Warren Photographic.

Table of Contents

Childhood

Claire Baker

If I Were a Child Again

If I were a child again
What would I see?
Well I'd rarely see reason
And think Mostly of Me.

I would do things without consequence,
Without fear of demise,
And I'd live my life
As One Great Big Surprise!

I would see the World
As a Spectacular Place,
And greet every day
As a Gift to embrace.

There would be no boundaries
Of where I could go,
How much I could do,
How much I could know.

Claire Baker

Nothing would faze me,

No stumble or fall,

I'd simply stand up again,

Six Feet Tall.

I would chase every dream,

There would be no refrain.

My love would be boundless,

No barrier of pain.

So follow your heart,

Whoever you may be,

Live your life to the full,

And set that child free.

*

But *Why?*

Mummy, why is the moon high in the sky?

Something to do with gravity dear –

It's hard to explain why.

But why mummy? *Why?*

Why is it so high?

Nanny, why are the birds all sitting in a row?

Well, they're gathering to fly away –

To go somewhere without snow.

But why nanny? *Why?*

Why do they have to go?

Well, if they don't fly away,

They'll get cold and won't grow.

Claire Baker

Daddy, why is the farmer in the den?

It's just a silly nursery rhyme son –

Dens aren't meant for men.

But why daddy? *Why?*

What is a den then?

Well, it's a place where wolves live –

Like pigs live in a pen.

Don't be silly daddy, silly!

Pigs can't live in a *pen!*

And daddy, why does the farmer want a wife?

That's a good question son –

She'll only cause him strife.

What's that daddy? Strife daddy?

Son, strife's a part of life.

Claire Baker

Look nanny! All the birds have flown away,

But they've left one behind –

Will they come back for him today?

Probably not,

But don't you dismay,

He'll fly off on his own

And catch them up on the way.

Look at the sky, mummy. Why is it so red?

Something to do with the weather dear.

Come on, sleepy head.

But why mummy? *Why?*

It's time for your bed.

But I'm not tired mummy.

You heard what I said.

Claire Baker

But, I want to fly – high in the sky,

Like a bird, like a plane,

Why can't I fly?

It's something to do with gravity dear –

It's hard to explain why.

Well mummy, please mummy,

Can't you *try?*

Alright my son, I promise to try

To explain those things

That aren't clear to the eye,

As long as *you* promise

Never to stop wondering why,

I'll do my best,

And I'll try to explain why…

Now close your eyes and go to sleep,

And pray the Lord your Soul to keep,

And dream of being a bird *so* high,

You can touch the moon right there in the sky.

Goodnight my mummy,

I'm flapping my wings high.

Goodnight my son,

Fly high, wondering why.

Claire Baker

Look at You!

Look at *You!*

With your big brown eyes
Telling no lies
Little floppy ears
No concerns or fears
Wet spongy nose
Whatever life throws
Always being there
Showing that you care.

Look at *You!*

Sitting in that chair
With that mighty air
Always on your guard
Tail wagging hard
Barking at the mail
Postman going pale
People passing by
Planes in the sky.

Claire Baker

Look at *You!*

One fluffy mass
Racing through that grass
Panting by that brook
Sniffing cow muck
Chomping on that stick
Stopping for a lick
Sniffing round that tree
Searching where to wee!

Look at *You!*

With your hairs everywhere
Not a single care
Waiting for a scrub
Bathing in our tub
Chewing guest pumps
Making smelly trumps
Gollopping down your food
And not being called rude!

Claire Baker

Look at *Me!*

Making lots of noise
Playing with my toys
Running round about
Making mommy shout
Trying to be good
But playing in the mud
Getting really dirty
Making dad shirty.

Look at *Us!*

We've met our match
Playing fetch and catch
Playing with our sticks
Trying new tricks
Digging in the dirt
Sometimes getting hurt
Falling on the floor
Playing tug of war.

Look at *Us!*

Running to and fro
Everywhere we go
Following each other round
Shouting at what we've found
Splashing in that puddle
Stopping for a cuddle
Asking for a treat
Something nice to eat.

Claire Baker

Look at Them

Curled up in the firelight,

Soft paws on nose, and fur held tight.

No stick, no bone, nor puddle in sight,

Just the gentle glow of the fire at night.

Exhausted from the day they've had.

No care of being good or bad.

In the other's company, never sad.

Forever friends, forever glad.

**

Claire Baker

Adolescence

This is *My* Life!

I can, I can't
I will, I won't
I think I should
But then I don't.
I ought to know
By now, I should
What's right
What's wrong
What's true
What's good.

I'm s'posed to know
The boundary
Of what to do,
To think and see.
I'm s'posed to know
The path to take
And if I don't
Just what's at stake.

I can't do right
I can't do wrong
Just one big battle
All day long.
I don't do this
I *do* do that
And all I get
Is shouted at.

Claire Baker

This isn't the time
To yell at me.
It's help I need
Can't you see?
You need to try
A different tack
And maybe then
I'd not talk back
But listen to what
You've got to say
To help me through
To find my way
To be the best
That I can be
Just stop for a moment
Stop nagging me.

Take a step back
And let me be
Stop forcing me
Stop rushing me
Maybe then
I'd start to see
Just what to do
Just how to be.
Have faith mom
Believe in me
Just tell me once
Then leave me be.
This is *my* life
Can't you see?
Let *me* decide
What's right for me.

Claire Baker

Men and Women

(Past 'butterflies' in the stomach, pre-children!)

Different Planets

"Is this alright?
Does it look ok?"
"Great" he said
(without looking her way).

"I'm not sure?" she muttered,
"Though I don't know why."
"It's fine" he said
(concentrating on his tie).

So she carried on getting ready –
pulled her boots to her knees.
He went downstairs –
checked the doors, got the keys.

Then he waited a while…
But she didn't appear.
So he called up to her,
"Don't be long, Dear."

And he waited a while longer…
Then shouted, *"we'll be late."*
"I'm coming, I'm coming.
It doesn't start till eight!"

Claire Baker

So he went outside
And opened the car door,
Started the ignition,
And then he waited some more…

When she finally appeared,
She'd forgotten her purse.
She went back inside.
(He started to curse).

When she came back out,
He wound the window down,
Muttered something,
Then started to frown.

"What's the matter with you –
What's with the staring?"
There was a brief pause…
"Is that what you're wearing?"

Claire Baker

What is it with Men?
(or God She's Annoying)

"Have you farted again?"
"No I haven't dear."
"Well it wasn't me
And nobody else is in here."

"Can't you do it outside?"
She said - airing the bed.
"I can't plan it like that.
It's involuntary" he said.

"No it's not!" she argued.
"You pushed that one out."
"Alright! Alright!
I'll control it, don't shout!"

A few moments later
He got out of bed.
"What are you doing?" she asked.
"Going outside like you said."

Claire Baker

So he stood in the corridor
And let one go.
(It was a fraction amusing
Though she didn't let this show).

He started to return,
But she stopped him mid-track…
"Don't come in yet
Or you'll bring the smell back!"

"For Pete's sake Dear,
I want to go to bed."
"Well if you fart again
You're in a separate bed" she said.

Too tired to argue
Or move to another bed,
He clenched his buttocks
And fell asleep instead.

Claire Baker

Claire Baker

Parenthood

Solitude No More

The Baby's crying again
I'm on the loo.
The paper's run out.
What do I do?

I reach for my dressing gown
Hanging on the door,
Find an unused tissue,
Drop it on the floor.

I stretch to get it
Without leaving the seat,
Fall on my knees –
My knickers round my feet.

The baby's now screaming.
The telephone rings.
And I lie there reflecting
What joy Parenthood brings.

Claire Baker

Pre-natal Dementia

We were going to be continental (we said).

Take the baby everywhere – no set time for bed.

"It's going to be <u>part</u> of our lives, <u>not</u> the centre".

Bo..ocks! We must have had some sort of pre-natal dementia.

But nothing fills the heart more,
and makes you feel so complete…

Claire Baker

A Mother's Love

I must kiss you a hundred times a day.

I can't help it. It's just the way

I feel about you deep inside.

Such deep emotion, I cannot hide

This love I have and sense of pride

Is overwhelming. You know, I cried

When you came into our world

When your scrunched-up body unfurled.

And from that moment on, my son,

You've given me so much joy and won

My heart forever. Forever I will be

In love with you, eternally.

Claire Baker

For Everything You Do, Dad

I must be the luckiest little boy,

You fill my heart with so much joy.

You tickle me and make me laugh,

You tell me stories in the bath,

You wipe my nose when it gets snotty,

You clean my face when it gets grotty,

You pick me up when I am teary,

You carry me when I am weary,

You cut my nails when they get long,

You tell me off when I do wrong.

But all the time you love me still.

And hold me close when I am ill.

You make me feel so safe and secure,

Each day I love you, more and more.

Claire Baker

How the World Feels Different when you've Had More Sleep

Wouldn't it be great to wake up naturally,

Instead of being awoken at the crack of dawn.

If we could just lie in bed until seven or seven thirty,

How we took sleep for granted before the children were born.

We're always woken up before six thirty-five,

And for every hour that follows we only feel half alive.

If we could just stay in bed for that little bit more,

We'd not take sleep for granted like we did before.

And now our eldest child won't go to bed when we say.

He keeps on getting up, trying to get his own way.

He's also waking up in the middle of the night,

And we've let him sleep with us, without putting up a fight.

We soon realised we should have put him back to bed.

We should have made more effort and been strict with him instead.

If we didn't clamp down it would be a hard habit to drop.

If we kept on letting him do it, it'd be difficult to stop.

Claire Baker

So, if he didn't go to bed or got up in the night.

We threatened to close his door and to turn out the light.

But with no natural wake up in over three years,

It hasn't really worked and we've all been in tears.

So we talked to our friends and we sought their advice,

And they kindly advised to go back to being nice.

To explain to him softly when we tucked him up in bed,

We'll reward him with stickers if he does what we've said.

Now after just one story when we turn out the light,

He quickly settles down – with his sticker board in sight.

And as for waking later – well there's not been a peep.

How the World feels different now we're getting more sleep.

Claire Baker

What About *Me?*

"Can I have this? Can I have that?"
"I don't want this, I want that hat."
"I'm hungry mommy, I want my tea."
"Quick mommy, I need a wee!"

Sometimes I find myself standing alone,
Away from the children in a room on my own.
Wondering whether this is it for me?
I no longer count. I'm a non-entity.

"I don't want this, I want that there."
"I don't want to sit here, I want the really big chair."
"But, I'm not tired, I don't want to go to bed."
I don't want to read that, I want this instead."

Sometimes I find myself staring into space,
Wishing Scotty would beam me out of this place.
I don't want to do the washing. I don't want to cook the tea.
I just want some time to do something for me.

Claire Baker

"Stop doing that! I've told you before."
"You've had enough. You can't have more."
"Did you do this? Well, who was it then?"
"You don't draw on walls! Give me that pen!"

I'm fed up with telling them what not to do,
of being followed around, no privacy on the loo.
I'm fed up with putting everything away,
Having no time for me at the end of the day.

I don't want to do the washing.

I don't want to cook the tea.

I want to shout out aloud

"WHAT ABOUT ME?!!!"

Claire Baker

It's a Race

It's a race against time to get there for nine,

Why do I always leave it so late?

I really should try to get there in time,

I should aim to get there for eight.

Then, maybe I'd be fine to arrive by nine,

Instead of always being late.

But I'd probably find, I'd have too much time,

And I'd rather be late, than wait!

Claire Baker

Lament of a Working Mother

Each day, Every day

keeps racing away.

When they're gone, I call after them

too late for them to stay.

And those moments inside

we should have shared together,

I missed them, I didn't see them.

Now they're lost forever.

Claire Baker

Love and Marriage

Men!

Men? They're infuriating,

They're only half there.

They never listen completely.

They're never fully aware.

You ask them a question,

But they haven't really heard.

In fact most of the time,

They haven't listened to <u>one word</u>.

When they lose something,

They can't see it for looking.

You give them a list,

They come back with nothing.

They promise to do things,

But easily forget –

It's just never the same,

as when you first met.

Claire Baker

You wait in hope,

That they'll pre-empt what to do,

But they never do anything,

The way you'd like them to.

So, you're always repeating yourself,

Telling them twice,

And they think its <u>You</u> –

that <u>You're</u> not very nice

when you finally lose it

over the simplest thing.

What they don't get is…

This has been brewing!

And it could easily have been avoided,

Without any intervention,

If they had simply given you…

THEIR <u>FULL</u> <u>ATTENTION</u>

Claire Baker

Together Forever

"You know, I can't understand why you keep on nagging,
I do quite a lot – I don't mind bragging,
Yet whatever I say, whatever I do,
Just never seems to be good enough for you."

"Look, it's not been easy since having our first child.
Always doing the organising drives me wild.
I know you're not lazy but I just wish you'd see,
What needs to be done and not leave this all to me."

"You know, you could be married to someone far worse,
Someone who would give you more reason to curse.
I really don't deserve it when you nag and shout,
And it's not really worth it – it just stresses you out."

"Look, we're always woken up at something past five,
And it's hard to be nice when you feel half alive.
I wouldn't get so mad if you did what you said,
But you always get distracted and do something else instead.
And no matter what you do, no matter what you say,
You'll rarely get it right - and do it <u>my</u> way,
Because we're just not made the same way you and me –
We'll always see and do things differently."

"You know despite all your nagging, I love you still,
Despite all our differences, I always will,
And although there are plenty more fish in the sea,
I truly believe there's no other fish for me."

"You know, despite all my nagging, I still love you too.
If you weren't in my life, I would always feel blue.
I also believe there's no other fish for me,
That together, forever, we were meant to be.
And I know deep down throughout everything we face,
No-one else could ever take your place,
And those words we once said will always hold true...
...Together, Forever, 'I will, I do'."

Getting Through Hard Times

How the World Feels Different When the Sun Comes Out

When you feel so alone you could break down and cry,

When you've hurdles to climb but you've lost the will to try,

When you feel so drained as if you're living in a drought,

When you feel so angry you want to scream and shout,

When you feel so broken you've got nothing left to give,

When life's so bad you've just lost the will to live.

When every day it's a struggle to get by,

When all you want to do is just curl up and die.

When you think you've reached that final straw,

When you simply can't take life's knocks anymore,

When you've lost all faith and there's nothing but doubt,

Something seems to happen when the Sun comes out.

Claire Baker

From behind a cloud it appears in the sky,

You can almost sense a smile, and a twinkle in its eye,

As the warmth of its presence starts to seep everywhere,

It's like you're being cuddled by a GIANT TEDDY BEAR.

It's like sucking on a lozenge that makes you breathe with ease,

(You know – one of those lozenges that makes you want to sneeze).

It's like being released from prison, running freely in the rain…

Wiping steam from a window – seeing clearly through the pane.

Things appear so much brighter – there's no need to feel so sad,

And you start to count your blessings – life just isn't that bad.

That feeling of dread, or that urge to scream or shout,

Slowly dissipates away when the Sun comes out.

Claire Baker

Isn't it Wonderful!

Isn't it wonderful

how a dog can lead a blind man

and make his life complete.

Isn't it wonderful

how the air, sun, wind and rain

can harvest fruit so sweet.

Isn't it wonderful

how a baby squeals with delight

when it looks into its mother's face.

Isn't it wonderful

how so very good you feel

when you finally reach that Place...

Claire Baker

…when you can take a step back and look outwards in,

and marvel at the world again, and everything within.

Oh, Isn't the morning chorus,

JUST GLORIOUS!

on the first few days of Spring.

Isn't life just Wonderful.

Every Second, Every Minute

worth LIVING.

Reminiscent of Retirement

Claire Baker

September Days

How I love September Days
When you think the Summer has gone,
But when you step outside
You feel the warmth of the sun,
And you start to relax
And forget concerns and fears,
As a gentle breeze
Softly brushes past your ears.

And the birds chitter chatter
As you pass them by,
And a distant plane
Mows the lawns of the sky,
Reminding you of places
You have recently been,
And unfamiliar faces
You have recently seen...

Of young children giggling
Building castles in the sand,
Their parents knelt beside them
With a loving helping hand,
By a deep velvet sea
Simply shimmering in the sun.
How I love September Days
When you think the Summer has gone.

Claire Baker

Claire Baker

Leaving this Life

Claire Baker

Brevity and Insignificance (of Life)

One

single blade of grass in a million meadows

single grain of sand in a thousand deserts

single drop of rain in the deepest ocean.

One solitary star.

That's all we are.

In the

flicker of a flame

ripple on an ocean

blink of an eye,

Our life passes by.

Claire Baker

Where are You, Nanny?

Nanny, where *are* you? Where have you gone?
I want to show you this hat I've got on,
And the hole that I've made with my stick in the lawn,
And this picture of you, and of me, that I've drawn.

Nanny, where *are* you? Why weren't you there —
At my Birthday today, when we went to the fair?
We had a big party, and ate a big cake,
But it wasn't the same as the cake that <u>you</u> make.

Where *were* you Nanny? Is it something I've done?
I wanted to show you the goldfish I'd won.
I really wish you had been there today,
I missed you Nanny. *Why* couldn't you play?

Daddy says you have gone to a place on the hill,
That although I can't see you, you love me still.
It's a place with a steeple and bells that chime,
A place where people sleep for a very long time.

Claire Baker

But, I'll miss you Nanny – the way you held my hand,

All the stories you told about a magical land,

The little songs you sang, when I was ill,

To calm me down, and keep me still.

I'll miss you Nanny – all the games that we played,

All the towers we built, all the pictures we made,

How you chased me around while I ran to and fro…

The gentle way, you loved me so.

Nanny, wake for a moment, for I want you to see,

This picture I have painted of you and of me,

I've drawn you with wings, like a butterfly,

And you're flying above me, high in the sky.

Claire Baker

I am Not

For everyone who has lost someone
and finds it difficult to let go…

Claire Baker

I am not

I am nowhere

I am not here

I am not there

I am nothing

I am no-one

I am no more

for I am gone.

There are no days

There are no hours

There are no birds

There are no flowers

There are no sunsets

There is no sky

There are no rivers

to walk on by

For I am not

I have ceased to be

I am no more

There is no me.

Claire Baker

But I once lived, breathed, felt and thought
And life was magical, mystical, fun and fraught…

I saw mountains, rainbows, sunsets and trees,
I felt the warmth of the sun and the ocean breeze.
I heard laughter, music, thunder and rain,
I felt hungry, thirsty, joy and pain.

And there were moments of magnitude – the miracle of giving birth.
Nothing ever surpassed this in worth.
I felt happy, sad, full of pride.
How we laughed, danced, sang and cried.

And there were times of regret – things said and done.
Silly arguments lost and won
Over work, money, material things -
Times we lost sight of the joy life brings.

But without any faults, there would have been no learning.
Without strays from the path, there would have been no journeying.
Without any sadness, happiness would not have felt complete.
Without any toil, rest would not have been so sweet.

Claire Baker

Now there are no more thoughts

There is no feeling

There are no words

There is no meaning

For I am gone.

I have ceased to be.

I am no more.

There is no me.

*

But I am still here

– in your memory.

Life is remarkable.

Do not grieve for me.

Claire Baker

Claire Baker

Epilogue

Stop to Smell the Roses

Remember Childhood

And how you once saw,

The World before you –

A wide open door…

…There were no boundaries

Of where you could go,

How much you could do,

How much you could know.

…The World appeared

A Spectacular Place –

Every day

A Gift to embrace.

…You chased every dream,

No concept of fate,

Your love was boundless,

No notion of hate.

Claire Baker

Well, Life *is* remarkable,

Too brief to waste,

In dispute, in argument,

In grief, or in haste.

So,

When days become blurred,

And start racing away,

Or some little thing

Starts to spoil your day,

Draw in the reins,

Change the gallop to a trot,

Put your foot on the brakes,

And take stock of what you've got...

Claire Baker

Take a stroll around the garden,

or a field, or a plain,

Walk barefoot on the grass,

Stand naked in the rain,

Hear the buzzing of the bees,

Watch the birds flying high,

Stop to Smell the Roses,

Don't walk on by.

And be here now –

One hundred per cent,

Don't ponder on the past,

Make time well spent.

Plan for the future,

But don't dream your life away,

Stop to Smell the Roses –

Make the Most of Every Day.

***

Claire Baker

Claire Baker

Claire Baker